WHY IS BILL GATES SO SUCCESSFUL?

Biography for Kids 9-12
Children's Biography Books

DISSECTED LIVES
auto biographies

D1214657

Speedy Publishing LLC

40 E. Main St. #1156

Newark, DE 19711

www.speedypublishing.com

Copyright 2017

Bill Gates is known for being one of the richest men in the world and the founder of Microsoft. In this book, you will be learning about his early life and how he was able to achieve these amazing accomplishments.

WHERE WAS HE RAISED?

He was born on October 28, 1955 in Seattle, Washington and given the name William Henry Gates III. His parents were William H. Gates II, a well-respected Seattle attorney, and Mary Gates, who was a teacher prior to having her three children. Bill had a younger sister, Libby, and an older sister, Kristi.

WILLIAM H. GATES

He enjoyed playing board games and was quite competitive at just about everything he did. Bill was an intelligent student and math was his best subject when he was in grade school. Bill, however, would easily get bored at school and would end up in trouble quite a bit.

His parents tried to keep him out of trouble by keeping him busy with outside activities such as Boy Scouts, where he earned his Eagle Scout badge, as well as reading science fiction books.

Once he turned thirteen he was sent by his parents to Lakeside Preparatory School in hopes that it would be more challenging for him.

PAUL ALLEN

This was where he met Paul Allen, who would become his future business partner.

COMPUTERS

There were no home computers like we have today such as the PC, laptop, or tablet, when he was growing up. Large companies owned computers and they took up a large amount of space. Lakeside school bought time that students were able to use on these computers and Bill found it all very fascinating. Tic-tac-toe was the first computer program that he wrote.

COMPUTER SET

Bill and a few of his fellow students were banned at one time from using the computer since they were able to hack it to obtain additional time to use it. It was then that they agreed to find bugs in the system in exchange for time to work on the computer.

While still attending high school, Bill devised a scheduling program for the school as well as a payroll program for another company.

In addition, he started a business with Paul Allen, a friend, authoring a program that helped with tracking traffic patterns in Seattle.

HIS COLLEGE YEARS

In 1973, after Gates graduated from high school, he studied at Harvard University. He originally planned to study law, but continued to spend a lot of his time on computers. He remained in contact with Paul Allen, who was now working at Honeywell.

Once the Altair personal computer was released in 1974, Bill and Paul decided to create a BASIC software program to run on the computer. They contacted Altair and advised them that they were working on this program.

Altair asked for a demonstration within a few weeks, however, they had not even started working on the program. Over the next month, Bill worked diligently on the program, and they eventually went to New Mexico for the demonstration and it ran perfectly.

MICROSOFT – THE BEGINNING

Gates dropped out of Harvard in 1975 in order to start Microsoft, along with his friend Paul Allen. Microsoft was doing well, however, it was a deal that Gates made with IBM in 1980 that would change the world of computing. Microsoft had reached a deal with IBM to provide the MS-DOS operating system for IBM's new PC.

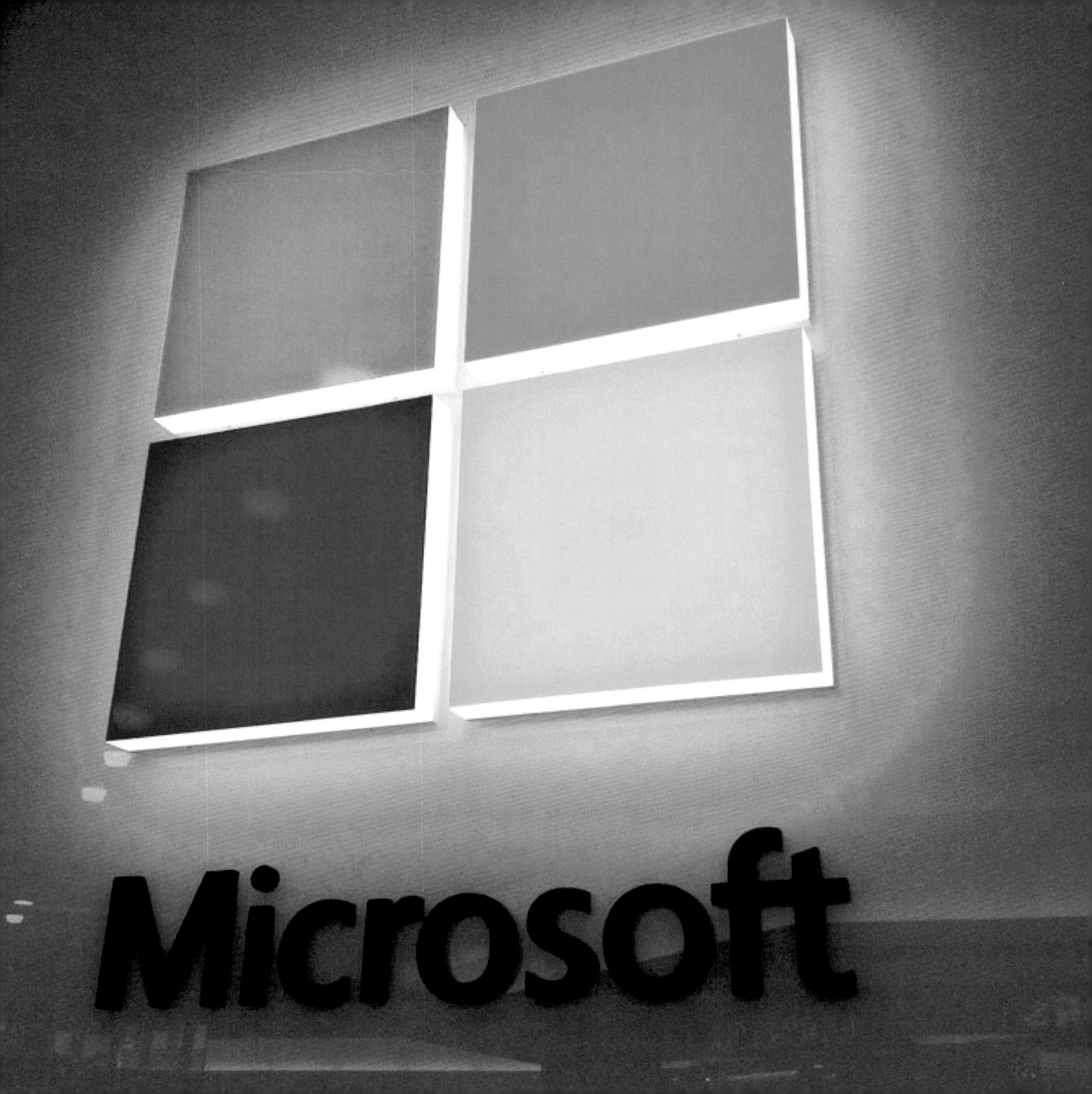
Microsoft

He proceeded to sell the software to IBM for $50,000 but held onto the software copyright. Once the PC market started taking off, Microsoft proceeded to sell MS-DOS to various PC manufacturers.

Microsoft was quickly becoming the operating system being used in a huge percentage of computers around the world.

WINDOWS

Gates and his new company decided to take another risk in 1985 with the release of the operating system named Microsoft Windows. This was their answer to another system that had been introduced by Apple in 1984. In the beginning, many people felt that Windows was not as good as Apple's operating system.

MICROSOFT® WINDOWS™

Version 3.1

MICROSOFT AND APPLE RIVALRY

Gates, however, continued to pursue the open PC model. Microsoft Windows had the ability to run on a variety of PC compatible machines, while its adversary, the Apple operating system, could only run on Apple machines. Microsoft won this battle and soon was installed on almost 90% of personal computers throughout the world.

MICROSOFT GROWS

Gates wasn't content with just winning the operating system area of the software market. During the next few years he introduced additional products for productivity called the Windows Office Suite that included Excel and Word. Windows Office programs like Excel and Word. In addition, Microsoft introduced new and improved versions of Windows.

WINDOWS OFFICE PROGRAMS

BILL GATES

THE WORLD'S RICHEST MAN

Gates took Microsoft public in 1986 and the stock was worth $520 million. Bill owned 45% of the stock, which was worth $234 million. Microsoft continued with its rapid growth, and the price of the stock soared. Gates' stock, at one point, was worth more than $100 billion. He had become the world's richest man.

HIS MANAGEMENT STYLE

From the company's beginning in 1975, until 2006, he was primarily responsible for his company's strategy regarding its products. He had become known to be distant from other people and as early as 1981, an executive of the industry made it known that "Gates is notorious for not being reachable by phone and for not returning phone calls."

Another one remembered that after showing Bill a new game and proceeding to defeat him 35 out of 37 times, when they met a month later Gates would win or tie every game.

Bill had studied the game until he had able to "won or tied every game. He had studied the game until he solved it. That is a competitor."

In the company's early years, Bill was active in developing software, particularly if it was on Microsoft's programming products. However, his role most of the time later was primarily as executive and management. He has not been on a development team officially since he worked on the TRS-80 Model 100, however, he continued to write code up to 1989 that was shipped in Microsoft products.

Tandy Radio Shack TRS-80 Model 100

Original Price: $ 799 to $ 899

1983

Base configuration:
2.4MHz 80C85 CPU, proprietary operating system in ROM, ROM socket, 8K RAM,
32K ROM, monochrome LCD, integral keyboard, RS-232C, parallel, cassette, and
bar-code ports, BASIC, application suite in ROM, internal modem, AC adapter,
slipcover

Important options:
Disk/Video Interface, external 3.5 or 5.25 inch floppy disk drive, carrying case

He continued to be interested in the technical details. Gates announced on June 15, 2006 that he would be transitioning from his day-to-day role during the next two years so that he could devote more time to philanthropy. He then split his responsibilities between two successors, placing Craig Mundie in charge of long-term product strategy and Ray Ozzie in charge of day-to-day management.

POST-MICROSOFT LIFE

Since leaving the day-to-day operations at Microsoft, Bill continues his philanthropy and works on various projects. In 2013, Bill was the highest earning billionaire throughout the world, according to the Bloomberg Billionaires Index.

STRENGTHENING GLOBAL FOOD SECURITY

SATYA NADELLA

Since January of 2014, most of his assets have been held in an entity known as Cascade Investment LLC, through which he owns part of several businesses, including Four Seasons Hotels and Resorts, and Corbis Corp. Gates stepped down from his position as chairman of Microsoft on February 4, 2014, to work alongside Satya Nadella, the new CEO, as a Technology Advisor.

WHY WAS HE SUCCESSFUL?

Similar to other successful entrepreneurs, Gates' success was achieved by a combination of intelligence, hard work, business sense, timing and luck. He would constantly challenge his employees to innovate and work harder, but he would also work just as hard, if not harder, than his employees.

He was not afraid to take risks. Dropping out of Harvard to start his company was a risk. Changing the operating system from MS-DOS to Windows was a risk. These risks, however, were calculated. He had confidence in his product as well as himself.

HIS PERSONAL LIFE

In January of 1994, Gates married Melinda French and they proceeded to have a son and two daughters. The Bill and Melinda Gates Foundation was formed in 2000 by Bill and his wife. This Foundation has become one of today's largest charitable foundations throughout the world. Gates has personally donated more than $28 billion to charity.

BILL & MELINDA GATES FOUNDATION
VISITOR CENTER

What is BASIC?

WHAT IS BASIC?

BASIC, which is an acronym for Beginner's All-purpose Symbolic Instruction Code, consists of a family of general purpose, high level programming languages whose emphasis is on ease of use.

WHAT IS MS-DOS

MS-DOS is the acronym for Microsoft Disk Operating System which is now a discontinued system that was used for x86-based PCs that were mostly built by Microsoft.

No PC Should Be Without It

MS

MS

MS

WINDOWS TECHNOLOGY

MICROSOFT WINDOWS

Microsoft Windows, often referred to as simply Windows, consists of a graphical operating system metafamily that has been created, marketed, and sold by Microsoft. There are many families of operating systems, and each one caters to a particular segment of the computing industry with the operating system usually affiliated with IBM PC compatible architecture.

Bill Gates is an intelligent man as well as a strong competitor, which is how he got where he is today. It simply took some time to figure out what he enjoyed doing and what he was good at. What do you think you would like to do? Are you a competitor? What subjects in school do you enjoy? These are all questions to consider when thinking about what you would like to do when you get older.

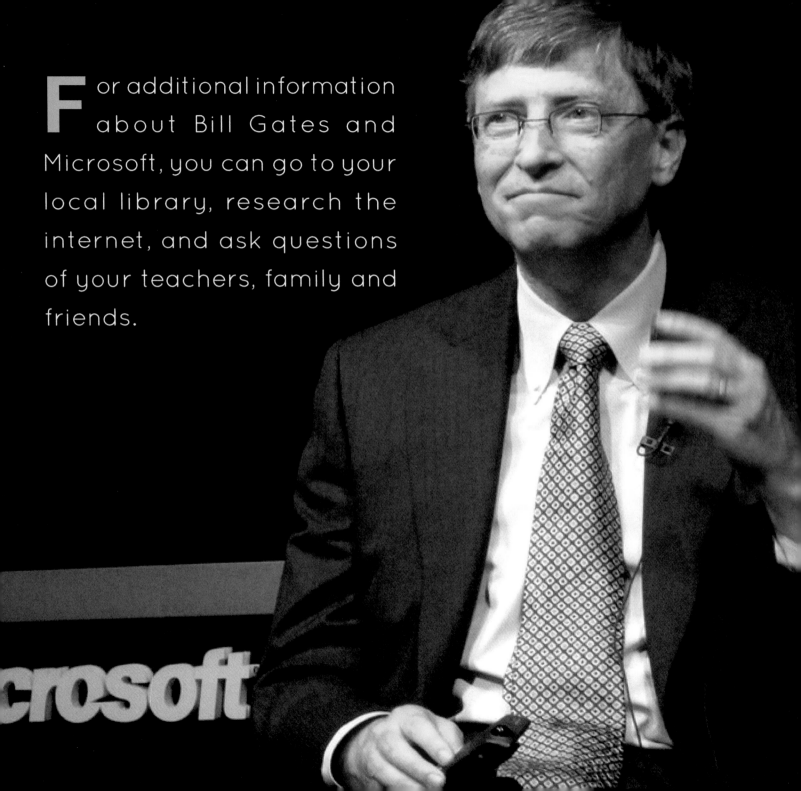

For additional information about Bill Gates and Microsoft, you can go to your local library, research the internet, and ask questions of your teachers, family and friends.

Visit

DISSECTED LIVES
auto biographies

www.DissectedLives.Com

To download more inspiring autobiographies and biographies
of great people from our website. Discover more about people
that changed the world during their time!

Visit our website to download more
Free eBooks and Get Discount Codes!

Made in the USA
Columbia, SC
28 April 2019